# THE

# PERFECT
# RESUME

FOR INFORMATION ON OTHER ASPECTS OF BUSINESS,
REFER TO OUR OTHER
WINGS PERFECT BUSINESS GUIDES
INCLUDING:

*The Perfect Interview*
*The Perfect Meeting*
*The Perfect Negotiation*

# THE

# PERFECT

# RESUME

## MAX EGGERT

**WINGS BOOKS**
*New York • Avenel, New Jersey*

*For Patricia Ann*

Copyright © 1992 by Max Eggert

All rights reserved.

This 1994 edition is published by Wings Books,
distributed by Random House Value Publishing, Inc.,
40 Engelhard Avenue, Avenel, New Jersey 07001,
by arrangement with Random Century,
an imprint of Random House UK Limited.

Random House
New York • Toronto • London • Sydney • Auckland

Printed and bound in the United States of America

Library of Congress Cataloging-in-Publication Data

Eggert, Max.
    The perfect resume / Max Eggert.
       p.    cm.
    Rev. ed. of: The perfect CV.   1992.
    ISBN 0-517-10139-4
    1. Résumés (Employment)  I. Eggert, Max.  Perfect CV.
II. Title.
HF5383.E42   1994
808'.06665—dc20
                                    94-6706
                                    CIP

8 7 6 5 4 3 2 1

# CONTENTS

THE EXAMPLES—COVERING LETTERS

# THE PERFECT RESUME

The perfect resume is the resume that achieves the interview—no more, no less. When the resume puts your name on the interview shortlist, it has done its job.

## WE START WITH A WORD OF WARNING

Without too much difficulty you can find lots of people only too willing to give you advice on how you should present your career in resume form. In fact, people who give advice on resumes are rather like economists—if you laid us end to end we might go to the moon and back and you would still be given different information. We differ because there are no rules about resumes, no absolutes, only principles and it is these principles which are the subject of this little book.

Some of the suggestions that follow you will love, others you will abhor. Please be selective because in the end you are going to be the person who will be writing your resume. It has to be your document and consequently you must feel both comfortable and confident with it.

## MAKE IT SPECIAL

The life of corporate and graduate recruiters is dull enough already without everyone's resume being the same. Make your resume unique and special: Take what follows as guidelines rather than ground rules, suggestions rather than shibboleths.

There is no bible or Ten Commandments on how to write resumes, but only ideas and concepts which have been proven in the job market by thousands of job hunters with whom I have been privileged to work.

You will receive as many different pieces of advice on your resume as the number of the people to whom you show it. Before you take the advice ask yourself the Quality Control Question:

> When did the person giving this advice last gain a job for themselves or for someone else on the basis of what they are telling me to do?

If their job success or experience is not recent, handle the information you are given with care.

# THE RESUME IS THE TICKET TO THE JOB RACE

The resume is not only the first thing the potential employer sees about you; more significantly it is the only part of the whole job selection process over which you as a job seeker have 100 per cent control. You can't control the availability of the sort of job you want, you can't control who gets shortlisted, you can't control the interview—although you might if you read another book from this series, *The Perfect Interview*. No, you can only control how you look on your resume.

## THE TICKET TO THE JOB RACE

Your resume won't win you the job because it is rare for anyone to get hired just on the strength of their resume alone, but your resume will get you the ticket to the job race. Your resume is the ticket to the candidacy, so it goes without saying that it should be letter perfect, neat, easy to read and well organized. Even if you achieved just that, your resume would be, in my experience, better than 60 per cent of those which are sent by job hunters today.

# LOOKING TO TURN YOU DOWN

Remember from the outset that at the resume stage of selection the recruiter is looking for reasons to turn you down and not to take you on! Advertisements these days are going to attract hundreds of applications, sometimes thousands of replies are not that uncommon.

As a recruiter, if I have a pile of resumes, my main task is to reduce the mountain of "job hopefuls" to a molehill of "job possibles." So that the maxim "when in doubt, throw it out" is very much used by recruiters.

**SEE ME, SEE ME!**
The recruiter always thinks that he or she is good at their job simply because it never emerges how good the person, whose resume has just been rejected, might have been. Recruiters never gain any negative information about potentially brilliant candidates they have passed over at the sort stage. So right from the very start your resume has to be special, and state in as many ways as possible "see me, see me."

# NO GAIN WITHOUT PAIN

"I get so fed up with writing my resume and then keeping it up to date" is a frequent cry of the job hunter. It is amazing that some people want to get a lifetime's career into a resume that takes less than one hour to write.

If you get bored with writing your resume just think how boring it is to read resumes day after day.

## EIGHTEEN MILLION RESUMES

Here is a simple sum:

$$\frac{20\% \text{ of } 1.5 \text{ million} \times 5}{500 \times 2} = 1,500$$

Let me explain why you should have this number in mind when you are writing your resume. Say there were 1.5 million people unemployed and looking for work. Say that just one in five bother to write a resume. And supposing they send off just five resumes a week for 12 weeks, that is one per day for the average time it takes to gain a job. That is a staggering 18 million resumes in any one three month period. If only half of those are sent to Fortune 500 firms, then that means that those firms are being sent something like 1,500 resumes a week. Now reading 1,500 resumes each week is what I call really boring. For your resume to have any chance of success, it has to be something very special.

Your resume has to be like a young plant in a tropical forest reaching up to the light. If it is to survive, it must use every tip and strategy that it can. In addition it must be realized that although there are no short cuts to the resume, the investment in time and effort will be well rewarded.

# HOW MANY RESUMES?

In an ideal world there should be one resume specifically written and customized for each job, but today's job market requires you to send off hundreds of resumes to potential employers because competition is fierce and quality opportunities are scarce. Consequently, the resume has to be somewhat ubiquitous.

In my experience the serious job hunter needs three basic resumes, namely:

1. A resume built around your present job
2. A resume aimed at the next job in your career
3. A combination of 1) and 2) above

**KEEPING TRACK**
Make sure you remember which resume you have sent to which employer. It sounds easy enough, but an amazing number of applicants forget. Some careful administration is needed here.

# THE WORDS

**Résumé**
From the French, meaning "summary".

For the job seeker a resume is a personal document outlining pertinent information needed by a prospective employer. It is to enable the employer to tell quickly whether or not a meeting would be worthwhile. If what is seen is liked, it will lead to an interview. If not, it won't and you and the selector will have both been saved the time and effort of an interview.

## BASIC REQUIREMENTS
As with most of life, there are no absolutes and resumes are no exception. There are things which work in the job market and things which do not. What follows are some practical tips and ideas which have justified their inclusion through trial and error in the job market. The resume serves three basic requirements:

- To highlight your value to a potential employer
- To provide a structure and a curriculum for the interview
- To act as a record of the substance of the interview

Writing a resume is not difficult but if it is to achieve its purpose it will require time, effort, reflection, creativity and determination.

Above all, the resume must be written with the potential employer firmly in mind. Authors write with their readers in mind, advertisers with their potential customers in mind, and so must you. You are selling your skills and experience in the job market, and you must ensure that your personal brochure presents you in the best possible way to your potential buyer.

# CORECT SPELING

I bet the heading on this page jarred! It is obvious that everything in the resume has to be spelled correctly but you would be surprised how many have mistakes in them.

When you are only represented by two or three pages of paper it takes just one small error for the selector to put you in the "Polite Turn Down" pile.

## WHAT SPELLING MISTAKES SAY ABOUT YOU
All sorts of things are incorrectly inferred from a spelling or typing mistake, including:

• You really cannot spell
• You are lazy
• You are inattentive to detail
• You want to fail
• You could not represent the company
• You do not really want the job

There will be enough reasons for the recruiter to put you in the "No" pile without you providing by misspelling or the odd "typo" an additional reason.

It is not enough to run the resume through the spell check. This will catch the spelling errors but not the "typos" and a typo will have the same effect on a selector as a spelling error.

SEW KNOW MOOR ARROWS!

# SHORT SENTENCES

Make your resume easy to read. That means short sentences. Long sentences are complicated. Long sentences are difficult to read. Short sentences can be skimmed quickly.

Unless you are going for a job as a writer, facts are more important than style. The tabloid press approach is the best. Short sentences have power. The active tense is best. Remember you only have 60 seconds to get your message across. Do not make the reader work. Make your resume easy to read. Use short sentences.

# POSITIVE AND MINUS

With a little bit of thought, it can be recognized that certain words are far more positive in their impact than others of roughly the same meaning.

For example:

*negotiated* is stronger than *liaised*
*managed* is more positive than *supervised*
*controlled* is better than *responsible for*

Once the resume has been written every word needs to be examined carefully to see whether another more powerful or positive equivalent can be used.

## A PASSIVE ATTITUDE

Generally speaking, the weaker words occur when the job holder is either passive or reactive to the work situation rather than in control of things.

Here are some more examples:

| | | |
|---|---|---|
| maintained | prevented | rejected |
| ordered | provided | revamped |
| performed | recommended | specified |
| prepared | rectified | supported |

There is nothing intrinsically wrong with these words, but they give the impression of a passive person, someone who responds to situations rather than initiating them. With a little more thought and research more positive synonyms can be found and used to create a completely different impression—it is not what you do but the way you present it!

# YOU HAVE THE RIGHT TO REMAIN SILENT

Remember, you do not have to tell the selector everything. One of the reasons that resumes fail is because they are far too long. Why is it that police forces around the world say "You have the right to remain silent?" Because the more you say, the more you will entrap yourself. In resume terms the more you write, the more reason you give the selector to turn you down.

So keep it brief. How brief is brief?—Well, as a rule of thumb, if you say it all in two or three pages at the most there must be something wrong. There are many advisers who would say that just one page is all it takes. My view is that the more senior you are, the shorter your resume can be.

Our consultancy record to date is a 17-page resume which we had presented to us. Not only was it 17 pages long, it was not until you waded through to page 16 that you discovered what it was exactly that the writer was currently doing.

## THE "MUST SEE" DECISION

The resume is a personal brochure and not your autobiography. How many product brochures tell you all the bad points as well as the good? Same with resumes; you need to give the selector only enough information to make the "must see" decision. No more, no less.

There are no absolutes, but a reasonable rule of thumb is a minimum of one page if you are a senior executive, two pages if not, and for everyone four pages maximum including a technical page if you are in engineering, computing or similar.

The resume is often used to provide a structure to the job interview. This purpose is frequently ignored or unappreciated by the job seeker. If you tell an employer you flunked out of graduate school then the employer will talk about your failure. It is in your best interest to include only positive information and not feed the interviewer with negative points.

So you have a good deal of freedom to leave out information. What do you drop? Well, first of all, anything that is negative. Negative information is best explained at the interview when you have at least a fighting chance of explaining yourself.

If, for instance, you were fired five years ago because you disagreed with your boss but have had a fantastic career since, there is no rule that says you have to declare your dismissal on your resume. If you get asked at the interview why you left the firm five years previously you can then explain the circumstances.

## USER FRIENDLY

People in the computer industry have a good phrase, "user friendly", and that is what your resume should be. Remember that at the resume stage selectors are looking for reasons to turn your resume down because they have so many applicants. So you should make your resume as attractive and as "user friendly" as possible. User friendly means easy to read, easy to work with and, most importantly, easy to say "yes" to. Just ask yourself if you were an employer what information would you want to see first out of the following personal details—education, interests or experience? It has to be experience (unless you are a recent school or college graduate), then education, then interests and finally personal information.

Reasons for this are in the questions that the prospective employers ask themselves when they want to hire you. The questions they ask are:

Has this person got the experience and skills I need? (i.e., about work history)

Has this person gained the appropriate qualifications or do they have the right intellectual capability? (i.e., about education)

What is this person like? (i.e., interests)

Who is this person? (i.e., personal details)

Only the really famous are hired because of who they are. Most of us are hired because of what we can contribute, so let us be "user friendly" and get this information across to the prospective employer as soon as possible in our resume.

What often happens is that on leaving college young people write the resume for the first time. From then on whenever they look for a job they dust off their old resume and add their most recent experience to it so that the document just grows and grows rather like Topsy.

Now you might think that this is an easy way of writing a resume and it is easy but wrong. After two or three jobs the resume looks like a paperwork Frankenstein with old bits of personal history sewn together. Much better is to write a fresh resume each time you decide to take a trip into today's competitive job market. No one would go to an interview dressed the way they did when they first left school or college, so why should your resume be any different?

Now how else can the resume be "user friendly"? This brings us to the next point:

## THE REVERSE CHRONOLOGY RULE

Let us get back to being user friendly. Ask yourself the question:

> "Which is more relevant to a prospective employer of my choice—what I did when I left school or what I am doing now?"

or

> "Where are the skills and abilities I am currently selling —in my current job or in the one I took when I left school?"

The most recent experience is for most people the most relevant to their job hunt. So use this by employing the reverse chronological rule when writing about career and achievements. Whilst talking about career, doesn't that sound better than "experience" or "work", and even better doesn't the heading *Career and Achievements to date* imply something strong in that it is saying,

> "This is what I've done so far but I still have much to give."

Everybody has "experience" but it sounds uninteresting on a resume. Achievements are far more powerful. We shall be returning to achievements later in the book but I want now to turn to some suggestions about the layout of the career section of the resume.

# LAYOUT: FRAMED

Sometimes resumes give the impression that they have been shoe-horned on to the page. The content could be excellent but the visual presentation is awful. In the better restaurants food is arranged on the plate to look as good as it tastes. Food for interviewers ought to be arranged using the same principles—to make it look attractive.

If you look at a picture which has been framed, the margin at the bottom of the picture is usually larger than at the top or the sides. Look at the two diagrams below:

*Figure 1*

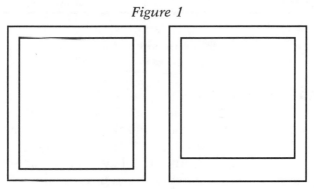

The one on the right is much more visually attractive. Lay out your resume in the same way.

**GETTING THE RIGHT LAYOUT**

Back pages of resumes are frequently only partially filled. This is a waste of an opportunity to be able either to add relevant information or to spread your information so that it appears more attractive.

Half close your eyes and look at your resume—does the block of information look lopsided? Play with the layout so that you gain a centrally balanced picture. See the diagrams below:

*Figure 2*

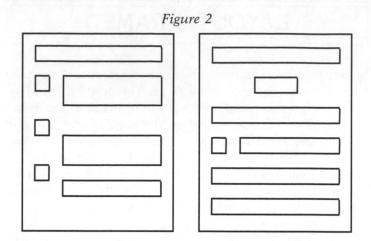

Again, it is the resume on the right which will create a better impression.

**EVERYTHING COUNTS**

Now, I know that it is nonsense to suggest that decisions by recruiters are made on visual impression and not on content. Of course, the content is by far the most important, but everything counts. If I have the job of sorting through six or seven hundred resumes and after I have been working for an hour or so I come across a messy resume which is poorly laid out, the temptation to move on to the next resume is often too great. Why should the selector spend time on your resume when the next one in the pile looks much more attractive?

Having worked hard on the content, make sure you present it in the most visually attractive way.

## 12

# TO JUSTIFY, OR NOT TO JUSTIFY

Unless you want to show off your word processing skills I would suggest that you do not right-hand justify your resume. There are several reasons for this.

First, if your resume is justified, it looks as if it is one of hundreds that you have produced. We know it is, but let the prospective employer think that your resume has been specially created and is original.

### AN OUTSIDER TRYING TO GET IN

Second, working documents in industry and commerce are not usually right-hand justified so when your resume arrives with its clean-cut right-hand margin, you are saying in a quiet way that you are an outsider trying to get in.

Finally, the ragged right hand edge looks more visually interesting than the boxed edge made by a right justification.

The best thing to do is to make sure that the resume looks good. Try two versions, justified and unjustified, and go with the one that looks better.

# QUALITY PAPER

Would you turn up to the interview in your weekend clothes? Of course not, but it is surprising how many people submit resumes on cheap photocopy paper, usually "borrowed" from their current employer.

Not that you are going to secure the interview on the basis of the quality of the resume paper, but image and first impression are increasingly important these days.

## PLAIN WHITE BOND

Your resume should be on white standard bond paper because that is what almost every organization uses today. For a PR or marketing job, perhaps a pastel or stronger color could be used, but it is safer with plain white bond of the best quality you can afford.

Do you really wish to have your personal brochure on cheap paper? No, you don't. Your bond paper should match your interview clothing in that it should be the best you can afford and that goes for the paper for the covering letters and the envelopes as well.

# DON'T NO. 1—REFERENCES

**DON'T INCLUDE A REFERENCE**

Job seekers often feel obliged to include references in their resume but it is obvious that any reference provided by the job hunter is bound to be friendly. Thus there is little advantage to the employer writing to a reference who has been nominated by the applicant. I have not come across an applicant yet who has invited a prospective employer to write to someone who will not provide a positive comment about the job seeker's work, attitude and disposition.

Employers are mainly interested in the relevance of your skills, experience and, more importantly, your attitudes, commitment and motivation. So while a member of Congress may be impressive, or a local elected official, police commissioner or other dignitary, they are not likely to be able to speak directly as to your suitability unless, of course, you want to go into politics or the police.

Consequently, if you feel bound to mention references then the simple statement, "References available on request" should suffice.

**MINIMAL INFORMATION**

Following court decisions against employers who gave a true, but damaging, reference to another employer about a potential employee, most employers, or their personnel departments, will only give minimal information. Employers are usually more interested in qualitative data than quantitative. How hard you worked, or what aspect of your work you found interesting or did well is far more telling than bald statements of your job title and how long you spent in that job.

For these reasons, most references are taken over the telephone and given off the record. In spite of the fact that most large firms have policies about not providing references except through the Personnel Department these rules are not always kept.

What would one of your previous bosses say about you if he or she was asked:

- What did he actually do?
- How well did he do it?
- What was her major contribution to the department?
- How did she get along with other people?
- Was he a self starter?
- Could she be left unsupervised?

Obviously the truth will out but you can certainly help the truth along in a variety of ways.

## YOUR IDEAL REFERENCE

After you have completed your resume a useful discipline is to write out your ideal reference for yourself. What would you like your previous boss to say about you? How could you justify all the points you wanted made about your work and your approach to it? Once you have done this, I would suggest you telephone your potential referees and bring them up to date with your career aspirations, plans and actions. (This is not always appropriate with present employers except in some public sector jobs where you are expected to move on regularly). Having told your referees about your plans you can then refresh their memory about your recollections of your performance, with statements like "You remember when I did 'x', you said it was good because . . ." will at least help them recall your good points. After you have spoken to them ensure that they have a copy of your resume as a reminder of all your achievements.

Particularly important when you want to change your career is to emphasize those aspects of your job and skills profile which are allied to your new sphere of aspirations.

# DON'T NO. 2—PHOTOGRAPHS

What you must remember here is that for most of our history as humans we have been swinging around in trees, painting mud on ourselves and eating each other. Our primal instincts have taught us to look at another person and very quickly form an opinion about that person. We think yes—no, good—bad, like—dislike. Although in certain states employers, because of discrimination rules, are not allowed to request photographs, some job applicants still like to attach a picture of themselves to their resume. My advice is that you should think about this carefully before taking this step. You see, opinions are highly influenced just on visual information alone. So unless you were blessed by birth by being in the top five per cent for traditional good looks and are photogenic, you're likely to fall victim to visual discrimination. If the research finds that traditionally good looking criminals get shorter sentences than ordinary looking criminals, then what chance have you got as an applicant if, like the rest of us, you are just average in the looks department?

The media is an industry committed to stereotype and image making. Every newscaster is both handsome and authoritative. Someone could be a ninety-eight-pound weakling and still be able to read the news, but I've not seen one yet. If you are just ordinary to look at, and most of us are, do not include a photograph.

## A PROFESSIONAL, NOT A BOOTH
If a photograph is called for then invest money on this aspect of the job search project. Passport photos are not good enough for resumes. Go to a professional portrait

photographer and tell him or her exactly what you want. Take along pictures from business journals or company corporate literature that you like and brief the photographer on the image you wish to project. Sometimes it is helpful to decide on three adjectives to describe the image you feel you have or you wish to project and tell the photographer that you want to look

competent, dynamic and hardworking
or
professional, thorough and reliable
or
creative, enthusiastic and dynamic.

Whatever three words suit you, and are appropriate to the type of job you are pursuing, ask to be photographed in a half smile. People looking at photographs of individuals with a half smile rate them as more intelligent, more friendly and with better interpersonal skills. The sort of things you would want in an employee anyway.

## HAVE GLASSES, LOOK INTELLIGENT
Secondly, if you normally wear glasses, wear them for the photograph because again you get rated as more intelligent than those who don't wear them.

Experts tell us that we should wear darker clothes to look more powerful. The point here, of course, is that you should think carefully about what you wear and the image or expectations it will create.

However, the basic rule still is: don't include a photograph unless you have to and if you must send a photo then spend money on getting it right.

# DON'T NO. 3—SALARY

The iron rule of wages says that employers will pay you as little as they can to get you, motivate you and prevent you from leaving. Salary, then, is a negotiation point and to get this in perspective we must take a small excursion into the rules of negotiation (because I presume you wish to gain as much salary as you can for your services).

The second rule of negotiation is "only negotiate from power" (the first being only negotiate with decision-makers). When you are one of 150 or so other candidates who respond to a want ad, you have no power. So then is not the time to mention salary or what you want.

When you get on the short list you are one of perhaps five people but this is still not the time to mention pay and conditions.

Now, supposing you are the last candidate in the ring, do you have power? You bet. If the prospective employer turns you down now, he or she knows that the whole recruitment process is going to start all over again and that is worth real money to you.

## AS LATE AS POSSIBLE

Always, always, always leave salary negotiation as late as possible in the selection process. Remember—if you start on a low salary with a firm you will stay low. One of the reasons for changing jobs is to improve your financial situation so employers expect you to negotiate. This point is covered in great detail in the book *The Perfect Interview*, but for the time being don't include a figure for expected salary on your resume.

You may be writing to one of those firms that gives a low

basic wage but lots of benefits—like a company car, stock options, your telephone bill paid and holidays which can be linked to business trips to the company's offices in the West Indies, Miami or Hong Kong. They are offering a basic of $35,000 plus all these add-ons. They see from your resume that you are earning $38,000 without all the benefits but do not short list you because you are earning too much! So please, don't include salary. If you insist on putting something then I would suggest the phrase "Salary is negotiable at interview."

## WHAT THE PROFESSIONALS REQUIRE

Sending your resume to agencies and headhunters, however, is different. These firms are paid a commission (sometimes as high as 35 per cent) of first year's earnings. They have a vested interest in getting as much for your "head" as possible. In the salary stakes they are going to be on your side, so provide them with details of current package and, of course, what you would like to earn. You will get the benefit of some realistic feedback on your market worth.

Letting agencies know how much you earn and how much you expect (or will move for) does not preclude salary negotiations with your employer.

# BE UNIQUE

If the employer writes the ad well and specifies exactly what is required then about 80 per cent of the resumes that are received will be from people like yourself who actually fit the specification. You will have had the same qualifications, the same sort of experience, so how can you appear different in a positive way? I would suggest from your achievements in a non-work situation—particularly if you have held an office or a position to which you were elected. For example:

Elected Treasurer of the College Geological Society
Elected Secretary of the PTA
Elected to the Committee of XYZ

What does this term "elected" mean? It says in a very quiet way—"Look, my peers and colleagues outside the work context think that I am reliable, honest, responsible and trustworthy enough to be elected to serve them in this or that capacity."

## SPORTING ACHIEVEMENTS
Now, not all of us hold public offices or are members of the Rotary Club, the Lions or the Elks—although, if you are, they are worth mentioning. What about sporting achievements current or past? Even if you are past fifty years old you can always tuck in somewhere that you represented your school or team at some particular sport.

I have worked on the resume of a Scotsman and a South African. The first acted as coach for the volleyball national team and the second was captain of a national youth team. Neither had his considerable sporting achievement on his resume.

What about your interests? You could put "reading", but how much more interesting if you put

The English Novel prior to 1930
or
Modern Autobiographies post 1952.

## THE SOCCER CLUB ADMINISTRATOR

I recently met a lady who had a very modest job in a lighting factory. Twenty years previously, because her son was fanatical about soccer and had no one to play with, she organized first a soccer team, then a league and is now administrator of the town's local soccer club which is affiliated to the national association. Now, if I were an employer looking for good administration skills, interpersonal skills and determination, her achievements outside work would say it all.

# MORE INTEREST IN INTERESTS

Just two more things on outside interests and activities. (Not too many, otherwise the employer might think that you will not have time for work.) What you spend your disposable income on or your free time on tells a potential employer a great deal about you, your values, your motivation and, in some cases, your intelligence.

For instance, supposing someone had as her interests

- Bridge at competition level
- Crosswords
- Software design

she is likely to be

- Intellectually able
- Good at problem solving
- Precise and possibly competitive.

Supposing someone had

- Squash
- Entertaining
- Restoring classic cars

he is likely to be

- Competitive
- Sociable
- Possibly practical.

## LET COLLEAGUES HAVE A SAY

What interests will you declare on your resume? Ask some friends at work—who do not know you socially—"What image does this create for you of someone?" and then give them your three interests. Is what they say the image you want to present?

Don't forget, the primacy rule works here as well. Here is an example:

Translating medieval German mystery plays into
   English
Television—especially drama
Family—enjoying my young children

gives a completely different picture to the following:

Family
Television
German translations

The last point on interests really applies to the whole resume. Remember interviewers eat what you feed them. If it is in your resume then be prepared not just to be asked questions about what you have written but to be tested to destruction.


## BE PREPARED—TO EXPAND

Woe betide you if you can't expand in detail on what you put down. Frequently, when I was a full-time recruiter, I would see that someone had put reading as an interest and then at an interview was unable to tell me quickly what was the last book they read. I once asked a young man to tell me about his interest in films, only to be told that he had seen a certain Clint Eastwood film all of three times. If you fail the credibility test in one part of the resume, it contaminates the whole resume. Just like those people at an interview who use the phrase, "Well, to be really honest . . ." and make you wonder about the veracity of the whole interview. Be prepared to talk fluently in the interview about your interests.

# THE WHOLE TRUTH

As I've said before, interviewers eat what you feed them and as most interviewers are not trained in this basic management skill, you can expect your resume to form the basic structure of the interview. It is absolutely paramount that everything on your resume can be verified and is true. If you cannot justify or speak about any part of your resume, your entire credibility will be lost and your chances of a job offer will be minimal.

**NO FICTION, PLEASE**
Omissions are permissible. That is to say, you can leave out negative information but be prepared to be challenged on the "gaps" during the interview.

Just as you would not wish to join an employer who lied about your salary or career prospects, by the same token you should not invent qualifications you do not have or fictitious employment. These things are easily checked and, even if you are hired, could be used as grounds for dismissal.

# USE THE BACK PAGE AND PUT IT ON THE RIGHT

If you must say something which is not in your favor, then here are two tips. First put the bad news on the back page; and second, put it on the right-hand side.

## PUTTING IT IN PERSPECTIVE

Put it on the back page so that at least the selector will read all the good stuff first, and any potentially negative information can be put into its appropriate perspective. For example, if the positions which you are applying for usually require someone of graduate school status, and you have no graduate degree but you have the appropriate experience, then structure your resume so that your career outline and details appears before the section on your education.

Now let me explain why the right-hand side of the resume should be used. Resumes are usually skimmed not read. They are gone through very quickly to gain a short list pile and a somewhat larger PTD (Polite Turn Down) file. When people skim for information, because they read from left to right, the left-hand side of the resume is read with far more attention and accuracy than information appearing on the right-hand side.

# CAREER SUMMARY

Constructing the career summary is perhaps the most important and significant preparation for the resume. Whether or not you decide to use a career summary in your final resume, it is still a very useful discipline.

A career summary is a simple statement of twenty or so words that encapsulates your career aspirations and what you wish to sell in the market place. Imagine that you only have thirty or so words to convince a prospective employer to listen to what you have to say. This process will concentrate the mind and focus the reader on what exactly it is you wish your resume to project.

The summary brings three potential benefits:

- First, it will help you become quite clear on which of your skills you wish to utilize and the shape of the career or job you want.
- Second, when placed strategically after your name, address and telephone number, it will act like a banner headline for your resume. In jargon terms, it acts as a pre-conditioning statement, that is, it conditions the reader to anticipate positive information about you.
- Third, a career statement can be used rather like a go/ no-go gauge in quality control. Everything that you wish to put on your resume should in some way support and justify the career statement. If you wish to include something about yourself which does not match the criteria of your career summary, then it may be wise to delete the item.

Developing a thirty-word career statement starting with a blank page can be quite a difficult exercise so you might like to try the following approach using a "mind map" and the "mnemonic" for the SAKE of your career.

**SAKE**
SAKE stands for the four different areas of yourself in which a prospective employer has an interest, namely your:

• Skills
• Attitudes
• Knowledge
• Experience

So here is the procedure:

1. Take a sheet of paper and put your name in a circle in the center and then from the circle four arms coming off with Skills, Attitudes, Knowledge and Experience (see figure 3).
2. Now, just think about yourself in these areas, in terms of what you have, what you have done and what you have to offer a future employer. Let your imagination ebb and flow, jotting down anything and everything that comes to mind.

You can show your mind map to your partner, to a good friend or a business colleague whose views you value, because we sometimes miss the obvious or even devalue what we have to offer.

3. Next, go through your mind map, first taking out all the things you don't want to do, or use. Having done this, then rank in order all those aspects about yourself a potential employer would be interested in. This will give you the curriculum for your career summary.

*Figure 3* Personal Career Statement

Develop a mind map for your career to date, using the structure below.

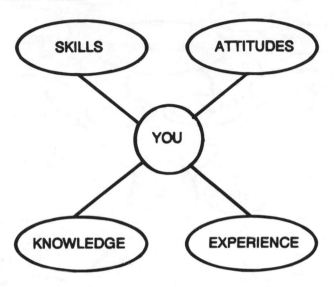

On the next page you will see an example of how this structure has been used by a computing specialist.

*Figure 4* Personal Statement Mind Map

By playing with these concepts this individual was able to develop the career statement overleaf.

4. Write your career summary in the third person singular as if you were an employment agency sending out details about yourself to a potential employer. (See below and Chapter 49.)
5. Continually revise your career statement until you feel comfortable with it.

## CAREER SUMMARY

A senior marketing professional with significant management experience gained with major U.S. and European high technology multinationals.

An effective thinker and doer offering proven strategic planning, business management and communication skills. Able to work effectively at all levels in organizations with the ability to manage change and achieve commercial profit targets.

Further examples of career statements can be found in Chapter 49.

# FIRST THINGS FIRST—AGAIN

If you were a prospective employer what would be significant if you were looking for an employee? Put these facts in order of importance:

- Who you worked for
- When you worked for them
- What you actually did

I'm sure you came up with the right answer, which is:

- What you did
- Who you did it for
- When you did it

And yet we rarely see the individual's career history set out in this way in resumes.

## SETTING IT OUT
It makes sense to put on the left-hand side what you did—recalling what I said about reading from left to right, put the important things on the left. In the center of the page goes the organization that you work for—you don't need the address at this stage, it takes up too much room—and the dates go on the right-hand side. If you have had lots of jobs and you are worried about seeming to be a job hopper, or if you are a parent who has had a career break, you are more likely to create a favorable impression this way.

## CAREER TITLES

You remember what I said about the eye skimming? Well, not only does it skim from left to right, but also from top to bottom. If on the left-hand side you just have a list of dates this does not convey very much information, but if I can see a list of career titles this creates an impression. In the following two examples, for instance, if I just skip down the left-hand side of the page and see:

1. Regional Sales Director
   Sales Manager
   Sales Rep
   Sales Administrator

2. D.P. Manager
   Operations Manager
   Senior Analyst
   Analyst/Programmer
   Programmer

At a glance a whole career unfolds, presenting the impression of a career which is still advancing and not of someone who only stays in a job a short while before moving on.

# 23

# ACHIEVEMENTS, NOT JUST RESPONSIBILITIES

People are sometimes too lazy to write their own resumes, and just crib one from their job descriptions by writing down all their responsibilities. I suppose that is better than nothing, but anybody can be given responsibilities. It does not really say what you did or did not do. You should also remember that when personnel departments write job descriptions they are doing so for use in pay grading and appraisal assessment, not so that an individual can get a job elsewhere. Who in their right mind would want a resume that includes information written by someone else? It is rather like trying to sell a product using the raw material procurement specification and not developing any sales literature.

When you write about your job, don't say what someone else asked you to do based upon your job description but say what you actually did and how good you were at it.

## THE ACHIEVEMENT PRINCIPLE

This we call the achievement principle. An employee may be responsible only for stock, but a reduction in slow moving stock of 17 per cent and inventory levels reduced by 50 per cent are achievements.

Taking charge of sales in the midwest is a responsibility; continually selling over target by not less than 15 per cent in any one period is an achievement.

Basically, what you are claiming by highlighting an achievement is "Look, I did this for them, I can do it again for you." Lord Byron said something along the lines of "If you want to know what a man will do in the future, look to his past." In psychology we say the best predictor of future performance is past performance. So what we are saying here is—make your resume achievement rich.

# 24

# ACHIEVEMENTS ARE FAB

There is a very simple process for getting your achievements down. It is called FAB—F stands for "Feature"; A for "Analysis"; and B for "Benefit".

**F FOR "FEATURE"**
First of all, list all the things that you have actually done in a job. All those special successes, the times when you thought to yourself, "I really did well there" or "I really earned my salary there." These are the highlights of your job. These are all the "F"s for "Feature".

**ADD IN THE NUMBERS**
Now, we must work on the A. A is for "Analysis". We must analyse the feature. What was it, how big was it, who was involved, what were the savings to the company? Ask yourself the question, "Is there any way I can get a number attached to the feature—a quantity, a percentage, anything that can be measured?" Reasons for this are both simple and obvious. If an achievement has a number attached to it, it looks more impressive, more credible and more understandable. For instance, we could take the achievement:

Supervised the research of microbiologists.

Let's work through that. How many microbiologists, what grade were they, what type of research, how did you supervise them? Working through this type of question we get to this achievement:

Supervised a multi-disciplinary team of eight graduate microbiologists, directing research into enzyme technology.

## Help the gatekeepers to say "Yes"

As a Personnel Manager in charge of recruitment, I might not know much about microbiology or enzyme technology, but I do understand the words multi-disciplinary and directing and the number eight. So not only does it sound more impressive, you help those people we call "gatekeepers" to say "yes". Gatekeepers are people like those in Personnel or Human Resources who control the gate through which candidates pass into the firm. They don't have the final say in who gets hired but they do have a power to say who gets seen.

So a quick recap: Which sounds better to you?

Supervised the research of microbiologists.

or

Supervised a multi-disciplinary team of eight graduate microbiologists directing research into enzyme technology.

I know which I would prefer.

## SELLING THE SIZZLE

Let's now deal with the B. This comes straight from an established sales technique which suggests that people don't buy features, but do buy benefits.

For instance, I don't buy my car because it is a Turbo version, has a sun roof and automatic locking, I buy it because:

I can accelerate quickly, have fresh air in the car on a hot day and when I park I can secure the car easily.

In other words, I want the benefits brought by the features, not the features themselves—so sell the sizzle not the sausage.

## SO—WHAT?
It does not always work, but in the achievements section you should try to get in as many benefits to the company as possible. Use a very simple mechanism to do this. Ask yourself the question "So what?"—"So what was the company able to do that it could not do before?" "So what was the advantage gained by the company as a result of this achievement?" Perhaps an example will help me explain. The basic achievement is:

Raised venture capital.

Add the "A" for "Analysis":

Raised $10 million venture capital from Europe and Wall Street.

Add "B" for "Benefit":

Raised $10 million venture capital from Europe and Wall Street, enabling the company to grow without the requirement to consolidate the European expenses on the U.S. balance sheet.

The Personnel Manager doing the initial selection might not know too much about balance sheet consolidations, but it sounds good, doesn't it?

## AN ENGINEERING EXAMPLE

Let's take an engineering example:

Here is the "F" for "Feature":

Analysed video systems for marketing.

Here is the "A" for "Analysis":

Analysed advanced video systems for computer orientated go/no-go decision for marketing.

Here is the "B" for "Benefit":

Analysed advanced video systems for computer orientated go/no-go decision for marketing, thereby giving technical approval for the company's most profitable product.

Listen to these:

"Reduced stock levels by 17.5 per cent, thereby releasing $500,000.00 into company cash flow."

"Assisted in clients' understanding of tax regulations thus improving customer relations."

"Improved debt collection time from 85 to 54 days thus ensuring maximum cash flow."

I'm sure you get the principle.

On page 48 there are some "Action words" to help you identify your achievements. Think about a job you have held, and put an "I" in front of each action word to see if it triggers an achievement. Not all the words will generate achievements but a significant proportion should do so.

# USE THE PAST FOR THE FUTURE

Wherever possible, use the immediate past tense or "aorist" form of the verb to introduce an achievement. The noun form or the participle form is not as powerful. (Don't worry, this is a book about resumes not English grammar.)

Here are some examples:

"Managed" rather than "the management"
"Improved" rather than "the improvement"
"Investigated" rather than "the investigation"

—i.e. the past tense rather than the noun.

And again:

"Designed" rather than "designing"
"Analysed" rather than "analysing"
"Directed" rather than "directing"

—i.e. the past tense rather than the participle. The past tense gives the impression that you have actually done something. It is completed, it is finished, it is achieved—which on a resume is the impression you want to create.

Just two more things on achievements before we move on.

Deleting the first person "I" makes it easier for you to give yourself proper credit without appearing over-boastful.

By using the past tense you don't have to keep using "I" because you can leave it out and replace it with an asterisk or star. The second point is that you can now indent your achievements on the page so that they stand out better and the eye of the reader is drawn towards them.

Here is an example:

Project Editor        American Digest        1990–Present

American Digest is the largest publisher of scholastic material in the U.S.A. My position was to manage the production of texts, magazines and multi-media instructional programs for the elementary school market. Main achievements:

- Achieved product goals through supervision of staff ranging from 12 to 23 on projects up to $250,000, including independent copywriters and freelance editors
- Conducted workshops for teachers so that . . .
- Won the Miller education prize for . . .

Note here the order: job then company then employment dates. There is a brief description of the job followed by the achievements which are indented and the "I" has been omitted.

## ACTION WORDS

| | | |
|---|---|---|
| ACHIEVED | ASSESSED | COMPOSED |
| ACQUIRED | AUDITED | CONCEIVED |
| ADMINISTERED | AUGMENTED | CONTROLLED |
| ADVISED | AVERTED | CONVERTED |
| ANALYZED | AVOIDED | CO-OOR- |
| ANTICIPATED | BOUGHT | DINATED |
| APPOINTED | BUILT | CORRECTED |
| APPRAISED | CAPTURED | COUNSELLED |
| APPROVED | CENTRALIZED | CREATED |
| ARRANGED | COMBINED | DECREASED |
| ATTAINED | COMPLETED | DEFINED |

DEMON-
  STRATED
DESIGNED
DETERMINED
DEVELOPED
DEVISED
DIRECTED
DOCUMENTED
DOUBLED
EDITED
EFFECTED
ELIMINATED
EMPLOYED
ENFORCED
ENGINEERED
ENSURED
ESTABLISHED
ESTIMATED
EVALUATED
EXCEEDED
EXECUTED
EXTRACTED
FORECAST
FORMED
FORMULATED
GENERATED
GUIDED
HIRED
IMPLEMENTED
IMPROVED
IMPROVISED
INCREASED
INITIATED
INSPIRED
INSPECTED
INSTIGATED
INSTRUCTED

INSURED
INTERPRETED
INTERVIEWED
INTRODUCED
INVENTED
INVESTIGATED
LEAD
LIAISED
LIGHTENED
LIQUIDATED
LAUNCHED
MAINTAINED
MANAGED
MARKETED
MODERNIZED
MONITORED
NEGOTIATED
OBTAINED
OPERATED
ORDERED
ORGANIZED
ORIGINATED
PERFORMED
PIONEERED
PLANNED
POSITIONED
PREPARED
PRESENTED
PREVENTED
PROCESSED
PROCURED
PRODUCED
PROMOTED
PROVED
PROVIDED
PUBLISHED

PURCHASED
RECOM-
  MENDED
RECRUITED
RECTIFIED
RE-DESIGNED
REDUCED
REGULATED
REJECTED
RELATED
REMEDIED
RE-ORGANIZED
RESEARCHED
RESOLVED
RE-VAMPED
REVIEWED
REVISED
RE-VITALIZED
SAVED
SCHEDULED
SECURED
SELECTED
SIMPLIFIED
SOLD
SOLVED
SPECIFIED
STAFFED
STANDARDIZED
STIMULATED
STREAMLINED
STUDIED
SUPERVISED
SUPPORTED
SURPASSED

| SURVEYED | TIGHTENED | TRIPLED |
|---|---|---|
| TAUGHT | TRADED | UTILIZED |
| TERMINATED | TRAINED | VITALIZED |
| TESTED | TRANSLATED | WROTE |

# RANK ORDER

Having used the FAB and "ed"s, we are in a position to list our achievements. Well, not quite. Just one more point, and it is another strategy that comes straight from sales.

A rhyming couplet that all good salesmen know is this:

> "If I can see the world through John Smith's eyes, I can sell John Smith what John Smith buys"

**WRITE FOR THE READER**

Apply this principle to your list of achievements. Looking at the list of all the things you have done, which do you think Mr. Smith, the recruiter, would like to see first, second, third, etc? For example, as an advertising account executive you might be most proud of your creative copywriting skills and thus at the top of your achievement list is:

Created concepts and wrote copy for . . .

but the job centers around good client management. This is what Mr. John Smith is looking for. So you should lead with:

Successfully planned promotions for blue chip clients

before giving any information about how creative your copywriting can be.

In rank ordering your resume, always write for the reader, our John Smith, and not for yourself.

# TELL THEM WHAT THEY WANT TO KNOW

Next important principle: Include only relevant information. If something does not support your career goal, then think hard about including it. Let me give you a personal example. I work now as a psychologist with organizations large and small, and mainly work with clients on the resolution of management problems. My first job on leaving school was working in a gin factory stacking bottles. My second job was working as an elevator operator in a molasses factory. My third was as a kitchen hand. Now on my resume this information would be true, it might even be interesting, but it definitely would not be helpful.

**RELEVANT INFORMATION ONLY**
My resume therefore would say:

> To enable self-funding through college a variety of casual jobs during the period 19__ to 19__.

I have only included relevant information.

We have seen resumes where people have given their social security number and their passport number—all irrelevant.

**LEAVE THE CHILDREN UNTIL LATER**
Frequently on resumes one sees the full names of their children, dates of birth and where they were born. When we challenged the writer of such a resume he justified

himself by saying: "But wait, the employer needed to know all this"—the answer is "Yes", but *not* at the resume stage. Remember the maxim—only enough information to get you the interview.

# KIDS' AGES

While talking about children—and this goes for men as well as women—if your children are at the ages 1, 2, 3, 5, 8, 10, 11, 13, 15 or 17, all those ages will ring alarm bells in the recruiter's mind because they are critical if a move or relocation to the new job is called for. The best place to explain what you are going to do about your children's education is at an interview and then only if it is raised by the interviewer.

## GROWN UP CHILDREN

Also, if you are older don't say you have two children aged 25 and 27; it just emphasizes your age. The recruiter who is just the gatekeeper might think to herself before she has even seen you, "Goodness, this person has children who are older than me."

# NO JOKES PLEASE, RECRUITMENT IS SERIOUS

Many people try to liven up the selector's day by injecting humor into their resumes. Don't be tempted. Don't be cute, chatty or funny. Selection and recruitment is a serious business. To be in the recruitment business is to be in a risk averse business like law or accounting—when it is easier for a recruiter to say "No" than "Yes", he or she usually says "No". By and large, recruiters always say "No" to humor. Not because they are boring people but because their own jobs depend on how successful they are at picking the right people. What do you think happens to recruiters who keep selecting the wrong people? They join the job market very quickly.

It is difficult to be funny in person, let alone on paper.

**MISFIRED HUMOR**
Here are some samples from people who have tried to be funny on their resumes. Under interests:

"Golf, golf and more golf"

Now, I'm personally not a golfer so I"m not too impressed by that.

Under main achievements:

"Wrestling with machine code and winning"

If I'm looking for a programmer, I would expect this anyway.

Basic rule: Don't try to be funny. Your resume should be serious if you want your application to be taken seriously.

# REASONS FOR LEAVING

Even in these days there is still an implicit understanding that people want and employers can provide lifetime employment. Maybe it is a hangover from the bygone age of the '50s and '60s when once you were employed by an organization you were there for life. Job hopping now as then was not thought to be good: It hints at instability.

## THE FOUR REASONS FOR LEAVING

Consequently, it is better not to include reasons for leaving on your resume. Such information can only serve to remind the potential employer that you are in control of your career rather than vice versa. Also, there are basically only four reasons why people leave jobs—better prospects, more pay, relocation or they were fired. Any of them, if the employer thinks about them seriously, makes you a potential risk as an employee—the question "will you stay" is raised by the first three and the last will almost guarantee you stay unemployed. It is better to leave such things to be explained during the interview, than to try to justify your career moves at the resume stage.

## HOW NOT TO GET AN INTERVIEW

The worst case we ever saw was on a resume that ran:

> REASONS FOR LEAVING: Dismissed: Due to personality clash with boss: Currently taking this employer to court: Confident of winning.

He came to us wondering why his resume was not producing any interviews!

The advice is, leave out "Reasons for leaving" from your resume. Explain it later in the selection process and then only on a specific invitation to do so by the interviewer.

# EARLY MISTAKES

If you were once a junior secretary and are now a Director of Advertising or Human Resources Manager, it is not going to be helpful to put your early job on your resume. If you were a lab technician before you became an accountant, or took your law degree part time while working as a janitor, it just does not help to include the more humble positions.

## RECENT JOBS ONLY

Most employers are mainly interested in what you have been doing recently. What you did ten years ago is unlikely to make a significant contribution to your next job. So where appropriate use summary statements such as "Prior to 19— a variety of junior jobs in engineering and retailing." Note we mention the industries not the job titles.

Sometimes a previous job is directly useful and then it should be included: a meat buyer who was once a butcher, for example, or a nurse who is now a Hospital General Manager are obvious examples of relevant experience. It was once said that the British car industry began to fail when accountants were appointed to run them rather than engineers who had shop floor experience.

You will have to decide for yourself how best to account for the early years of your career on your resume. The basic question to ask is: Does it fit and/or support my present career aspirations? If it does not help you in any way, then it should be omitted.

# EDUCATION

Your education successes should be set out employing the same principles as in the career section. Please do not make your employer hack through your primary and secondary education if you have a degree or a higher qualification. Consequently, the reverse chronological rule applies just as much to education as it does to your career.

In the same way your degree is more important than where it was gained, which is more important again than when it was achieved. The number of resumes where the date of the degree is given first is quite amazing. For those outside the "golden decade", this can only accentuate your age—"Gosh, this person was in college before I was born!" Also, in today's world of rapid change most science degrees are obsolete in terms of usable knowledge after about a decade. What is being sold is not the things you know about but the intellectual, conceptual and analytical abilities which you demonstrated in order to gain the degree.

**THE "TOPSY CURVE"**
What frequently occurs up to the age of 30 is what is called the "Topsy resume," because it just grew. This is a graduate resume which was written on leaving college and then subsequently added to prior to each job move. Thus a "Topsy resume" gives as much weight to the grade point average at college as it does to the achievements of the last job. With a little thought it becomes obvious that newly qualified job seekers need to provide lots of information about their studies because they have nothing else to offer. Once someone has had some work experience the empha-

sis must shift to this area. Employers, except in academia and not always then, are more interested in what you can do for them than how well qualified you are. Sometimes this is difficult for the highly qualified to accept. Just ask yourself the question, "If I was about to be treated in an emergency, who would I prefer to undertake the operation —a recently qualified surgeon who had not performed the operation before, or a paramedic who had successfully completed the procedure many times?" The latter, of course. Ideally one would like qualifications together with the successful experience but given a choice, experience wins every time.

## RESISTING AN EDUCATION!

This is why those without formal academic qualifications, if they have been successful in their careers, should not worry about not having degrees and diplomas. Employers prefer experience. Yes, of course, there are the professions where graduate degrees are a prerequisite for a job, but in the wide world of work, professional jobs are a small fraction of the total. In fact, although I would not recommend this as an excuse not to gain qualifications, most entrepreneurs from Alan Sugar to Richard Branson to the late Robert Maxwell seem to do rather well without the more traditional formal qualifications. Sometimes, it takes a good brain to resist an education!

To return again to your qualifications, your major or the courses you took in college. If you are pursuing a career in the sciences do not list your courses thusly:

English, English Literature, History, French, Geography, Math, Chemistry and Physics

It is not as impressive as

Math, Physics, Chemistry, etc

Lead with the most appropriate first.

# 33

# HEALTH

Should you tell your prospective employer about your state of health? You could take the view that how healthy you are is your own private concern. But it is obvious that the employer wants employees who are at work rather than off work with some malady and drawing sick pay. Consequently, if you are healthy, say so, for it can only be in your favor. "Excellent" is the word which most frequently appears on resumes, though I am not sure of the difference between good health and excellent health.

If your health has not been good then my advice is not to say so on the resume. The fact that you are returning to work must mean that you are currently fit for work, but this is the sort of information which is far better discussed at an interview. If I have two candidates whose resumes offer the same skills and experience, but one candidate confesses a significant health problem from which he has fully recovered and the other does not (although he too suffered from the same illness), it is obvious which one will be given preference for the interview.

## AN ILLUSION OF GOOD HEALTH
A way of creating the illusion of good health is to include some reference to a sporting activity among your interests and, if possible, a sporting achievement, no matter how long ago. It shows that you were fit and healthy at one time in your life with the implication that you are still fit now.

Employers are, for obvious reasons, biased against the weak and the sick, no matter how fit they are now. The best place to justify your fitness for the job is at the interview, not at the resume stage. So if you are healthy say so; if not, then omit this information.

## WHERE DISABILITY IS A PLUS

The exception is if you are disabled. In my experience employers positively discriminate in favor of those who are disabled. If your disability does not have a direct bearing on your job, then it is almost a guarantee of an interview.

If you have an obvious disability my advice would be, whether or not you declared it on your resume, to advise your potential employer before you go for the interview. If you attend interviews in a wheel chair or have a false limb and this has not been mentioned on the resume it is likely that you will be remembered for your disability rather than the skills and experience you can bring to the job irrespective of your suitability.

# 34

# GIMMICK RESUMES

Do not be tempted to use gimmicks. If your resume needs a special gimmick to gain attention, rather than your achievements or skills, then although your resume will be noticed it will not pass closer scrutiny.

If your resume is markedly different in paper color or typeface it says quietly, "I'm an outsider trying to get in." A gimmick resume gives the same message even more clearly.

**THE RESUME AND THE TRAIN TICKET**

Successful exceptions are few. A gimmick resume that worked was for a traineeship in the creative department of a famous PR and advertising company. Here the applicant did a one-page resume, had it miniaturized and gummed to the back of a weekly commuter train ticket, and sent it with a one-line covering letter which read,

Look what you can have if you fund one of these each week.

It gained an interview and the job. A Quality Control Manager put his resume onto the back of a quality award certificate his company won under his direction. The accompanying covering letter began, "To have a certificate like this displayed in your atrium to impress your clients . . ." Again, this worked, but by and large gimmick resumes provide a little welcome humor and diversion in the recruiter's humdrum day and little else. Would you buy a car because of flashing lights in the show window or select a restaurant for a celebration dinner because of the chance of winning a weekend holiday? Like you, employers are essentially traditional and sensible in their buying habits and not influenced by the superficial. Keep your resume normal.

**DISK RESUME**
If you want a computing job in a small or high tech company, putting your resume on a disk used to be a popular approach which began like, so many of these things, here in the U.S. However, since the advent of computer viruses many firms have strict policies about the use of floppies when their pedigree and form are unknown.

# 35

# COPING WITH BIAS

Now I am going to say something which may offend. Recruitment is an unfair process. Fortunately we are moving towards equal opportunity and there is much good legislation and more of the same in the pipeline. Still there is a gap between what should happen and what does happen.

The basic rule is to put any information about yourself which ignorant, biased and small-minded people could use against you onto the back page of your resume.

Names, for instance, tend to be country and culture specific. There are very few Smiths in West Africa and few Adebambos in the Midwest. If you do not hold a U.S. citizenship then don't put that fact immediately after your name. If you have a foreign-sounding name but you look like an executive in the Fortune 500, then use a photograph, irrespective of my earlier advice.

Discrimination and victimised prejudice are more easily proved at interview than at the initial papersort.

**AN EXTREME EXAMPLE**
In England, which is supposed to have the oldest judiciary and the mother of parliaments, I work with an Ethiopian woman who graduated from Oxford University with a good honors degree. She was fluent in English, French and Italian as well as several dialects of her homeland. The facts are these. She sent 150 resumes to graduate recruiters and had no invitations to interview. She anglicized her name and remailed the 150 resumes and achieved 10 interviews. There were only two variables—her name and the time she sent her resume.

You can choose to call yourself by any name you wish providing it is not your intention to defraud. Maybe John Smith and Fred Bloggs are having a hard time and a zero response from their resumes which they are circulating in Ethiopia.

## AN EVEN MORE EXTREME EXAMPLE

Again in England we were working as consultants with a young woman who held very strong feminist views, she objected to putting her marital status on her resume. In the end we persuaded her to do 50 resumes with her status and 50 without. I regret to report that it was the latter that generated more interviews. We have repeated the experiment several times since and achieved the same response.

It is a difficult decision. If one has to go to these lengths to get a job with a company, would you really want to work for that company anyway?

In making these suggestions and giving these examples we in no way support, encourage or condone prejudice in any way. It is our belief that once the best people are running our organizations, irrespective of sex, race, color, ethnic origin or creed, then equality will be a reality, but the first task is to get good people through the doors of prejudice which are, unfortunately, closed shut in many organizations.

# 36

# WHAT TO LEAVE OUT

As the resume will form the basis of the interview, and negative information at an interview always attracts more supplementary and probing questions, your resume should contain only that which is positive about you. So here is a section about what you might like to leave out. Of course, you must be prepared to answer questions in these areas at an interview, but at the resume stage your maxim should be:

"Yours to know and theirs to find out."

## AVOIDING PREJUDICE

Birds of a feather flock together, similar fish school together and wolves pack together. Recruiters are no different. They like to recruit in their own image. Most recruiters are WASPS—that is, white, anglo saxon and protestant. They are also married with 2.3 children, living in suburbia and buy their clothes from the large retailers that provide the uniforms of life. If you are different in any way from the norm, then it is a sorry fact of life you will experience prejudice in one form or another. Throughout human history this cloning process has gone on. In some organizations in an attempt to enforce an "us and them" regime, employees are expected to wear the same color clothing as the armed services. Further, many firms still make their employees wear uniforms and/or have dress codes. This is but the formalization of a natural process which for humans no longer has survival value. We don't have tribal warfare anymore so I can afford to look like myself and allow others to do the same. This lesson has, however, yet to be learned in many organizations and thus you may be screened out at resume stage.

So any information which can give rise to bias, facilitate prejudice or incur negative judgement from the ignorant should be left out at this stage of the selection game.

It is an indictment of our present society but if you are single, black, gay, politically active in your free time, failed your law exams the first time around or have dual U.S./Nigerian citizenship, your chances of getting an interview with a big city law firm anywhere in the western world are slim, irrespective of how brilliant your career and achievements may be.

## SUGGESTED OMISSIONS

Here are some of the things that we have discovered invite prejudice from the ignorant who abuse their power and discredit their organizations by their actions in turning good candidates down.
(Those marked with an asterisk* are dealt with specifically elscwhere in the book.)

- Examinations you have failed
- Your health, if poor*
- Major illness, both physical and mental*
- Junior jobs irrelevant to your present career thrust*
- Employment of less than a year
- Reason for leaving employment*
- Dates of degrees*
- Ages of children*
- Marital Status—if female*
            —if gay
            —if single and over 30
- Children, if adult*
- Period(s) of state detention
- Past labor union status—unless you are going for a job in industrial relations with a union or in politics

- Dangerous or "different" interests, e.g. hang-gliding and bungie jumping
- Nationality—if not American securing work permits is extra unwanted and difficult work for employers
- Political affiliations
- Place of birth if not in U.S.A.
- Fluency in languages of no direct use within the Western world or to the job on offer
- Higher degrees if the jobs for which you are applying have no need of them
- Your current salary and benefits*
- Your anticipated salary and benefits*
- Your photograph*
- Your references*
- Your career ambitions/objectives unless you are a recent graduate
- Anything that makes you look extreme or different

# BUT I'VE ALREADY SENT OUT MY RESUMES TO LOTS OF EMPLOYERS

Do not worry if you have bought this book after sending out your resume, because resumes have a shelf life of at most about two weeks in the mind of recruiters. Your resume might get put in the potential candidates file but either way you can always send it again on the pretext of having updated the document for the employer. Many a time in my experience an employer has seen a candidate on the "new improved" resume whereas there was a nil response to the original document.

# RESUME DON'TS—AGAIN

- Do not list your last salary or your salary requirement.
- Do not disclose why you have left your previous jobs.
- Do not list addresses of the firms you have worked for.
- Do not give the names or job titles of the people you worked for.
- Do not use "I" unless really necessary.
- Do not use jargon.
- Do not use abbreviations which will not be understood by all the potential recipients of your resume.
- Do not have any spelling or grammatical errors.
- Do not send photocopies.
- Do not use cheap paper.
- Do not use extreme type faces, silly visual effects or a brochure format.
- Do not include a photograph.

# APPLICATION FORMS

You will find it very frustrating if, having spent hours on crafting your resume and sending it off with the perfect covering letter, the only reward for your labors is an application form.

While this may be frustrating, remember two things. First, not everyone gets an application form so your resume has done its job. Second, no application form I have yet seen gives the applicant scope to write everything that is appropriate. This means your resume can still play its important role in gaining the interview.

## HOW RECRUITERS USE THEM

Employers use application forms rather like the army uses uniforms—they position everyone. It is easier for recruiters to interview from an application form because they know where to look for what they want, whether it be experience, personal details or expertise. It is helpful when you are trying to keep up the rapport to be able to glance down to a certain position and know that that section on the form will give the required information. Hacking through a resume at an interview mitigates against rapport and a natural flow to the conversation.

## FOR FURTHER INFORMATION . . .

Employers will not shortlist you if you return the application form over which you have printed, however neatly, PLEASE SEE RESUME. You must complete the form: but in doing so you can write at the bottom of various sections, particularly those detailing experience and achievements, FOR FURTHER INFORMATION PLEASE SEE

MY RESUME, which, of course, you have enclosed. (Please do not expect employers to have kept your previous resume or documentation.) It is no guarantee that your resume will be read again but you have given it your best shot.

# WHAT NEXT?

Once the resume has been written it must find its way to as many appropriate desks as possible. It is surprising that so many people spend ages constructing their resume and then don't send it to anyone, as if the invitations are supposed to come by some form of osmosis.

**LEARNING TO "PYRAMID"**

To whom should you send your resume? Here you have to learn to pyramid—as in pyramid sales. Your resume needs to go to someone who:

1. Can offer you a job
2. Refer you to someone who can offer you a job
3. Can tell you of a job opening
4. Refer you to someone who can suggest a potential job
5. Can give you the name of someone who can do any of the above

### THERE IS NO LIMIT

Getting a job is a process of being turned down. Getting an interview is about telling as many people as possible that you are looking for the next stage in your career. If your resume stays on your desk at home, so will your career.

# WHO CAN GIVE YOU A JOB

"Spend as much time as you can with prospective customers" is a basic rule of sales. Salesmen who spend all their time at their desk writing reports, talking to their design and manufacturing people and generally staying in house are unlikely to be successful because none of those people is likely to buy their product. It is the same for the job hunter—who is going to give you a job? It is not:

Family—they can give you support
or
Friends—they can maybe tell you of openings
or
Agencies—they can only submit your details on your behalf
or
Personnel Departments—they can only shortlist you.

It is only decision makers in appropriate firms that can give you the job you want.

## PICKING UP THE $50.00 BILLS

If an eccentric millionaire passed you on the street scattering handfuls of $50.00, $20.00, $10.00 and $5.00 bills there would soon be lots of people, including yourself, picking up the paper money. The best strategy would be not to pick up as many bills as possible but to collect as many of the high denominations as you could. In this way you would maximize the gains. Job search should follow the same principles. Most people just write to agencies then sit back and complain that:

a) they have heard nothing

b) agencies and head hunters are hopeless

c) agencies cannot understand your technical expertise

(Although the latter might make you feel good when you have just had your ego dented by needing to change jobs.) It is only employers who can give someone a job, so they are the equivalent of the $50.00 bills. Of course, your letter will be regarded as junk mail by most of them but you are more likely to be successful here than working with the other categories (the lower denominations in cash terms).

John Courtis, who runs his own excellent head hunting firm, sends a standard letter to job searchers—it makes the point so well that I have set it out in full on page 105.

The moral is simple: *Spend most of your energy contacting the most likely employers.*

# COVERING LETTER

Remember the equation on page 5. Not only does it apply to the resume but also to the covering letter. In fact more so, because the covering letter is the packaging for the resume. If the letter does not command the attention of the selector then why should he or she go on to read the resume.

Here are some obvious basics.

First, where possible it should be typed. Most written business communications are typed; if your letter is not you are signalling quite clearly to your future employer that you are an outsider trying to get in.

## DON'T SPLIT THE INFINITIVES!

Of course spelling and grammar should both be correct. Split infinitives still annoy people. You must remember that at this stage in the selection process it is only your letter and resume that contain information about you and who wants an employee who cannot even present him or herself correctly?

I would suggest that you do not right-hand justify your letter. As with the resume, it gives the impression that this is a standard document (which, of course, it is) that you have sent off to hundreds of potential employers (which, of course, you have).

See Chapter 44 for further advice on letters.

# TO WHOM?

Your letter must go to a named person. "Dear Sir/Madam" is an insult. Until you secure the interview your letter has the status of junk mail. If you begin "Dear Sir/Madam" it is more likely to be treated as such, and will probably not even reach the decision maker. Secretaries are paid to file junk or unsolicited mail vertically under W.B. If the *Readers Digest* can reach you by name and personalize the correspondence, you can do the same, so write direct to the likely decision maker by name.

## FINDING THE RIGHT NAME

The decision maker is likely to be your potential boss's boss. It is usually quite easy to find out the name of the appropriate recipient just by telephoning the receptionist. Some organizations, like banks, pharmaceutical companies and defense organizations have policies about not giving information over the telephone, in which case go to one of the directories (in any reference library), find the appropriate director and ask them or their secretary. Tell them that you want to send some information to the person responsible for the xyz function, would it be the director (or his/her secretary) to whom you are speaking? This usually prompts a "No" and that it should go to Mr. or Ms. so-and-so.

If you are a director or a senior executive then write to the chief executive by name. They are probably inundated with unsolicited mail from job hunters but if you have a skill profile which might be useful they will respond appropriately. The letters on pages 102 and 103 are real examples and proof that the system works.

## THE PERSONNEL DEPARTMENT

Giving you this advice will alienate my friends in Personnel and H.R. Departments. Being responsible for recruitment and selection, they naturally expect all job hunters' correspondence to be directed to them. However, good and professional as they are, Personnel Departments are but gatekeepers, albeit important gatekeepers, in the selection process. Personnel selectors can only say "No," they cannot say "Yes." It would not be fair to talk about monkeys and organ grinders, buttons and shirts or oily rags and engineers, but the principle is the same. It is only if you want a job in Personnel or Human Resources that you should write to that department, important though it is. Always write to the person who can give you a job.

# COVERING LETTERS

# 44

# STRUCTURE OF THE COVERING LETTER

The purpose of the covering letter is very simple: It is to get the recipient to read your resume—no more, no less. Although this is obvious and simplistic, it is surprising how many covering letters

- Are too long
- Repeat the content of the resume
- Are written from the applicant's point of view
- Contain negative information

and besides all this contain spelling and grammatical errors.

To my mind and in my experience, the covering letter needs only three paragraphs:

**1st Paragraph**    From the recipient's viewpoint or benefit give your reason for writing.

A good way of ensuring this is to use the sales letter strategy of beginning this paragraph with the word "Your".

For example:

- "Your advertisement was of great interest . . ."
- "Your company enjoys an excellent reputation in engineering . . ."
- "Your article in *Business Week* . . ."
- "Your recent results . . ."

Employers are bound to be interested in what is happening from their viewpoint.

| **2nd Paragraph** | To customize your resume and direct the reader to some unique selling point which meets or hits a specific need of the potential employer. |

For example:

- "You will see from my enclosed resume . . ."
- "Customer Services has been the main thrust of my career . . ."
- "Last year I won the largest widget order in the North East . . ."
- "Being a Unix specialist who is fluent in German . . ."

| **3rd Paragraph** | This is to ask for the interview, although interviews are work for personnel people. So we translate this into "discussion" or "meeting". |

For example:

- "The opportunity of a discussion . . ."
- "The chance to meet with you . . ."

Finally, this third paragraph is to prompt the reader into some form of action, thus:

- "I look forward to hearing from you"

or, if you are applying for jobs where some degree of confidence and assertiveness is required or expected:

- "Perhaps I may telephone your office next week to see how you may wish to proceed . . ."

You will notice that this is the first and only place where tentative language is used, "Perhaps I may . . . ," "to see how you may wish. . . ." This just takes the aggressive edge off the intention. For the most part, with cold letters your call will not be welcome but in today's climate no-one will think ill of you if you work hard at getting a job. Remember, if there is a potential position for you your call will be welcome.

You will find examples of how to end your letter in Chapter 45.

What follows are some tips and strategies and what not to do in the Covering Letter and some suggestions as to how they could be improved. We begin with three examples of what not to do.

## EXAMPLE I—WHAT NOT TO DO

*123 Main St.*
*Hometown, New York*

*May 26, 1994*

*Dear Sir/Madam,*

*I have seen your advertisements in various publications and feel that you are ideally placed to help me further my career.*

*I am an experienced Computer Customer Service Professional, and I currently work for one of the leading companies in the field. I am looking to expand my experience by moving to another company.*

*I would welcome an opportunity to discuss my experience and any potential opportunities with you. I will call you next week.*

*Yours sincerely,*

*Mr. P. I. Maxin*

### Comments
From someone who is in customer service this is dreadful. Here are some of the errors:

1. "Dear Sir/Madam"—This is almost saying "I don't care who you are and I'm too lazy to find out."
2. Every sentence begins with "I"—the writer sounds like an "ego" maniac.
3. The whole letter is written from the viewpoint of what the potential employer can do for the applicant. In retailing terms this letter is almost the equivalent of a

shopkeeper putting up a sign in his window saying, "Shop here so I can make a profit on you."

4. "I will call you next week"—There is a difference between assertiveness which is essential in getting a job these days and naked aggression. This bald statement is just rude!!

6. "Mr. P. I. Maxin"—he *must* be an egoist. It is not customary to put the appellation Mr. (or Ms., Mrs., etc.) in front of your name. If you must do it, then put it after your name in brackets.

## EXAMPLE 2—AGAIN, WHAT NOT TO DO

*Dear*

*I write in reference to our recent telephone conversation.*

*I enclose my resume for your consideration. I am aware that its presentation is not ideal and I am working on an improved format.*

*I have enjoyed a successful career in engineering, including management, training, counselling and sales/marketing activities.*

*I am interested in the possibility of becoming an associate in such fields as . . .*

### Comments
This was a letter sent to our consultancy. It was handwritten and not at all easy to read.

1. Ideally your covering letter should enjoy the same style and typeface as your resume. If this is not possible then do try to have it typed. If it is handwritten, since most of the world of work communicates on paper by the typed word, your letter signals clearly that you are an outsider trying to get in.
2. "I am aware that [my resume] is not ideal"—This is amazing! What is the implication here?
   —I can't be bothered to update it
   —You are not worth the effort of the re-write
   —This application is less important than other things I have to do

It would have been better not to allude to the paucity of the resume than include this statement.
3. "I have enjoyed a successful career"—implications of this should be thoroughly thought through. This phrase implies to me that the writer is now retired and no longer making a positive or significant contribution.

4. ". . . in the possibility of . . . in such fields as . . ."
   Instructions on how to write sales letters make a signifi-
   cant point about tentative language. In covering letters
   it makes you sound unsure or uncertain. Phrases and
   words such as the following might usefully be omitted:
   —I feel
   —I think
   —I might
   —Perhaps
   —Only
   —Just
   —It may

   Unless, of course, you deliberately wish to appear tentative (see comment number 4 in Example 1).

## EXAMPLE 3—THIS IS THE WORST EXAMPLE

*Dear Mr.*

*Here are five reasons why you should employ me:*

*1. If you do not, one of your competitors will.*
*2. Leadership qualities, both verbally and by example.*
*3. A refusal to accept second best in life.*
*4. Major achievements, mostly in the future.*
*5. In possession of a healthy body and a healthy mind.*

### Comments

In fact, the original had 11 reasons and the above represents an abbreviated version.

There is nothing wrong in making your covering letter different or being assertive or pushy but this is just silly, coming as it does from an MBA student. Even the points are open to question, for example:

1. What is a verbal leader?
2. How can you sell future achievements if you have no track record?
3. Employers take as a given that employees are healthy.

This list could be offered by most applicants. There is little which is unique here. If you wish to try this approach, which sometimes works, then a strong client orientation, coupled with creative and individual uniqueness is a must.

Now for some better examples of what you should do.

## EXAMPLE 4

*Dear*

*Engineering costs are a significant overload. For appropriate control, good management and best manufacturing methods are vital.*
*May I help in this important area?*
*My extensive skills and experience cover:*

* *Engineering management in "blue chip" companies*
* *Planning and executing capital investment programs up to $5 million*
* *Reducing labor costs in a union environment*
* *Introducing effective machine maintenance*

*The opportunity to discuss with you how my knowledge and ability could be used to your advantage would be most welcome.*

*Yours sincerely,*

## Comments
This letter, which was sent cold to possible employers, won an interview and subsequently a job, so the letter did what it was supposed to.

1. Notice how this letter, in comparison to Example 3, continually has the needs of the employer in mind and uses tentative language in the right place to soften the assertiveness.
2. The letter begins strongly with a statement which every manufacturing company would support.
3. Personally, I would have strengthened the selling points by:
   a) Using the past, e.g. "Plann*ed* and execut*ed*"

b) Quantifying the reduction in labor costs and the machine maintenance
c) Made more of the potential benefits to the employer.

Next is an example of how to present a non-traditional career.

## EXAMPLE 5

*Dear*

*What do candy and lighting have in common?*

- *BOTH NEED TO DELIVER MAXIMUM CONSUMER SATISFACTION*
- *BOTH NEED THEIR BENEFITS COMMUNICATED TO THEIR TARGET MARKETS*
- *BOTH NEED TO GENERATE A SATISFACTORY PROFIT FOR THE COMPANY*
- *BOTH HAVE BENEFITED FROM MY DIRECTION*

*As an experienced Marketing Director, I have a proven record in the management of change, resulting in increased customer satisfaction and an improved company profitability. My resume which is enclosed demonstrates this.*

*I am happy to supply further information or meet for a discussion when examples of my achievements can be matched more closely to situations in your organization.*

*Yours sincerely,*

### Comments
This is another cold letter to target employers.

1. This job seeker makes an advantage of a career background which is not normal, i.e. from confectionary to lighting products, in an interesting way.
2. The offer of "examples of my achievements" is also an additional reason why an employer might want to see you. You obviously have more chance of getting the job even if the interviewer initially only wants to see you because of your "examples."

## EXAMPLE 6—LETTER TO HEADHUNTER

*Dear*

*There is a legend that memories only last three months. I contacted you in the summer and am enclosing another copy of my resume to update your records.*

*I would like to convert this piece of paper into a face and look forward to meeting you.*

*Yours sincerely,*

### Comments

This gained several interviews when the first resume, which was written before the writer had advice, achieved a nil response.

1. Headhunters receive hundreds of cold letters a day. They usually begin with a very boring "'I was a senior executive with . . . ,'" so you can see how this effort was refreshingly different.
2. The last paragraph here is really interesting and provocative and I can see why it worked.
3. Most job seekers think that headhunters and agencies have hundreds of jobs on their books—they don't. Yes, they do use their contacts to secure assignments, but most of them do what most job seekers should be doing for themselves: contacting employers direct. My advice is be your own headhunter, representing yourself.

Headhunters, however, receive hundreds of unsolicited letters each week. See the advice of John Courtis in Chapter 47.

## EXAMPLE 7—IN RESPONSE TO A WANT AD

*Dear*

*The ability to steer the xxx Co. through an increasingly more complex and competitive marketplace.*

*The experience to understand intimately the requirements and opportunities for commercial sponsorship of the arts.*

*The stature to lead a prestigious organization and represent the xxx Co. at the highest levels of Industry and Government.*

*The skills to position the xxx Co. for optimum and profitable success.*

*The creative sensitivity to balance the artistic and the commercial requirements of the xxx Co.*

*If my understanding of the requirements for the role of Managing Director of the xxx Co. is correct, then you will find I certainly fit the bill! My attached resume details the bare bones of the success I have built as Managing Director and as President of the Industry Federation.*

*I look forward to an early opportunity to demonstrate how my particular skills and experience could be used to build and sustain the success of the xxx Co.*

*Oh yes! I trust that boundless energy and enthusiasm combined with an all consuming passion for classical music would not count against me?*

*Yours sincerely,*

**Comments**
This was written to a leading orchestra company in response to an advertisement.

1. The writer has attempted to get behind the words of the ad to demonstrate that, although his background is in a totally different arena, he can identify the issues and has the skill and experience to address them.

2. The last line just hints at the disposition of the man behind the letter. (He did not get the job but he got an interview, although there were hundreds of applicants.)
3. In the original letter there was one split infinitive and one typo, but in this case the writer was forgiven.

## EXAMPLE 8

*Dear Mr.*

*Your paper machine quality control systems and distributed control systems have been formidable competitors to our products in South East Asia and Japan for several years now.*

*I have for some time been expecting the same competition from your excellent company in Europe and it is interesting to note that you are not more active in the European paper markets than you are.*

*Should your strategy be entering the European market for paper machine control systems I can be of direct assistance.*

*As you will see from my attached career resume I helped establish Accuracy as the leading supplier of quality control systems to the paper industry in Europe and have in-depth knowledge and experience of this market in the UK, France, Holland, Belgium and Germany, as well as being trilingual.*

*My more recent experience includes the introduction of both the xx and yy Master systems to the paper and other industries.*

*Mr. W. W., President of ZZ Corporation, who is a long-standing friend and colleague from the days when we worked together at BBB, suggests I write to you directly.*

*Perhaps I may telephone you in the next few days to determine when a convenient meeting can be arranged for us to discuss the opportunities which the European Market presents for you and the start-up assistance I could provide.*

*I do hope a brief meeting will be possible.*

*Yours sincerely,*

## Comment

This was a cold letter. It did not gain a job but it did gain for this very able executive a two-week consultancy assignment in Japan.

Do your potential employers' thinking for them. This is an excellent example of an applicant who has done a wonderful job of doing his potential employer's thinking for him and then sold himself as the ideal candidate.

# 45

# EXAMPLE ENDINGS

It is surprising how many job hunters have difficulty ending their letters. Here are some examples, all of which come from letters that have won interviews:

- I would be pleased to meet you to discuss how I could contribute to your organization.
- I would welcome the opportunity to discuss with you how my knowledge and ability could be used in your company.
- I hope there might be an opportunity for a personal discussion.
- This letter and my resume provide the basis of my career achievements, but I would be pleased to flesh them out at a personal meeting to see if there is an opportunity to work with your company.
- I am frequently in New York and can be contacted at 212-555-1234.
- If you think it would help, I would be delighted to meet you to talk about this.
- My resume is enclosed. I would welcome a letter or your call to my office.
- I live locally and would be pleased to discuss with you, at any time convenient to yourself, the position advertised or any other that will enable me to provide input and benefit to your organization.
- I attach a note summarizing my background and experience. I should, of course, be glad to come and see you. May I call to find out if a meeting could be worthwhile?
- A phone call to my office (212-555-1234) will reach me,

or a letter to the above address. My resume is attached. I hope to hear from you.

- My resume is attached and if you would like to see me I should very much like to see you.
- Might not do any harm, at least to talk, if you have a mind to. My resume is enclosed and I hope to hear from you.
- I look forward to your reply and if there are any work areas upon which you require further information do not hesitate to contact me.
- The broadly based interests I have developed would quickly allow me to raise my knowledge to specialist level in a number of fields—a bold statement but one you might be satisfied with if we would meet.
- If I may, I will call your secretary next week to see if it is convenient for me to see you.
- I would like to meet you so that I can elaborate on these bare facts and answer any questions. I look forward to hearing from you.

# 46

# DO COLD LETTERS WORK?

Put simply—yes when sent to the people who can give you jobs—i.e. employers. The best analogy I can give is that of oranges: Everyone has bought oranges at some time. Greengrocers always display their fruit in the window or outside. Hundreds of people walk by every day and some purchase oranges. However, everybody needs oranges at some time. Job applicants should send out their resumes to anyone who might be able to offer them a job. Just as the greengrocer displays his oranges in front of potential purchasers, you should do the same with your resume. The grocer might hope that everyone will buy his oranges but he is not surprised or disappointed when people don't. Job seekers should have the same outlook.

On the following letters are extracts, with names which have been disguised, from actual letters leading to an interview which was gained from a cold application. Good covering letters do work!

**EXTRACT I**

*April 2, 1994*

*Dear Mr. James,*

*Many thanks for your recent letter and enclosed resume. As I am sure you are well aware, we do not currently have any vacancies at the moment, but nevertheless I have circulated your documents around some of our key managers, and should there be any relevance in talking to you, then you can be assured that we will follow up your approach to us.*

*Yours sincerely,*

*Miss Cathy Admin*

*cc James Bigman*
*Managing Director*

**EXTRACT 2**

*April 10, 1994*

*Dear Mr. James,*

*Further to my letter dated April 2nd 1994, the comments of my colleagues are that we do not have any suitable opportunities for you at BBB. However, we are quite impressed by your skills profile and it occurs to us that this may be of interest to one of our associated companies XYZ Company. I have, therefore, passed your resume on to them.*

*Yours sincerely,*

*James Bigman*
*Managing Director*

# 47

# A HEADHUNTER SPEAKS

What follows is a letter from John Courtis of John Courtis & Partners Search and Selection. The letter was sent in response to a cold call to his firm. What John Courtis says makes such sense that the letter, with his permission, appears in full.

*Dear*

*Thank you for your letter and resume. None of our current assignments matches your background and experience. Nonetheless we'll keep your resume on file with pleasure.*

*However, I am not sure that we are likely to be much use to you. What you have gained is entry to a sort of lottery. The reality of our existence is that we react to what our clients ask us to do. We can't predict what that is likely to be, even for a record like yours.*

*If you consider the criteria attached to any search or selection assignment you'll recognize that there are almost endless permutations of industry, sector, qualification, age, experience, location and so on. Actually, we receive over ten thousand applications per year but only handle a few hundred jobs.*

*Add to this the fact that our client list is finite and we are one of many consultancies providing recruitment services, so the odds against a perfect match with you are long. We'd love to help; if only because, when you've got a new job, we hope you may become our client.*

*My colleague, John McManus, tends to offer ancient wisdom on these occasions. Tell them to write to people who've got jobs to offer, he cries—they're called employers. He doesn't put it prettily, but he's right. Targetting chief executives within your area of competence is likely to be more productive. After all, if a job doesn't exist and they like what you say, they can invent one. We cannot.*

*Yours sincerely,*


*John Courtis, FCA, MPIM*

*P.S. Despite what some advisers say, we would appreciate an indication of your last salary. There are practical reasons for this. You can tell us what lesser sum you'd accept too, if it's appropriate.*

# THE EXAMPLES

# RESUMES

# 48

# THE STRUCTURE OF THE RESUME

There are some traditions and expectations about the structure of resumes, but it is more important that you develop a structure which shows off you and your talents to their best advantage.

The traditional structure, popularly known as "tombstone," is as follows:

Name
Address
Telephone number
Interests/Health
Secondary education
College and graduate school
Professional qualifications
Employment history
(in chronological order)

Our consultancy has not found this structure as successful as:

Name
Address
Telephone number
Career statement
Career and achievements to date
(in reverse chronological order)
Professional qualifications and training
College and graduate school

Secondary education
Interests
Personal details

We think this structure achieves more interviews because it delivers information to the potential employer in the order that it is required to make the decision whether or not to interview.

## QUALIFICATIONS

Employers are going to be more interested in what you can do in terms of skill and experience before you tell them how old you are or indeed what your interests are. We advocate, for those with recognized and job-relevant qualifications, that these are put after the individual's name on the basis that the employer can see immediately that you are a college graduate or that you enjoy an appropriate professional qualification. The education section can then go after your career because the reader already knows what you have achieved in this area.

There is an old adage that it takes "a good brain to resist an education." If you have made it to a senior position through a rigorous education in the university of life and hard knocks, then leave the education section out altogether. As we have said elsewhere, employment is about what you can do for an employer and not about how many certificates you can put up on the office wall.

What follows are some examples of various types of resumes. Some much better than others. Please use them as guides where appropriate and do not be tempted to copy. In our experience, applicants who crib chunks from the resumes of others have greater difficulty with their interviews: they have problems substantiating other people's achievements!

## EXAMPLE 1—WHAT NOT TO DO

*Curriculum Vitae*

Name:           David John Applicant
Address:        15 Main Street
                Newark, NJ
                12345
Telephone:      201-555-1234
Date of Birth:  April 4th 1946
Place of Birth: New York, NY
Nationality:    USA
Marital Status: Married
Children:       Two aged 10 girl
                          14 boy
House:          Owner
Car:            Owner/Driver
Passport:       Holder
Interests:      Music/Photography, Film Making,
                Mountaineering, Sound Equipment

---

### QUALIFICATIONS

1963   B.A.: New Jersey State University. Major: English
       Language, English Literature, Minor: Mathemat-
       ics, Science, and Technical Drawing.

1968   Ordinary National Certificate, Electronics and
       General Engineering courses (Sutton College).

1969   Apprenticeship with Kent Transformers Ltd with
       part degree course at N.E.L. Polytechnic.

1976   Digital Electronics Engineering Course, High
       Power Ltd, Newark.

1980   Analogue Data Analysis Short Course, Johnson
       Ltd, Newark.

1983    Data Signal Processing Seminar, Monologic Ltd.

1986    Management Training Course, XXX Ltd (Brighton Polytechnic).

*INDUSTRIAL EXPERIENCE*

*1974 to 1979*

Project Engineer
Optic Power Inc.

—Trouble-shooting on site at the Strand Theater, of Scenery Hoist Control Systems. Including Analogue computing and 415 Volt, 6 Phase Thyrister drive systems.
—Customer presentations and Systems training. Including Digital computing and power drives.
—Specialist power servo products Site Engineer. Including on site problem diagnosis and customer liaison.
—McGuire AFB, Aircraft wind tunnel development and site engineer. Including Installation Commissioning and testing of computer controlled 415 volt 3 phase drive systems.

*1979 to 1985*

Principal Systems Engineer/Project Manager
Exim Command and Control Systems Ltd.

—Overall responsibility for up to twelve engineers.
—Management of Control System development (systems, real time software, and servo engineering).
—General Systems Engineering. Including planning of trials and controlling a team to analyse results.

—Systems Engineering enhancement program to introduce improved technique for weapons control, including man-machine interface aspects.
—Development activities on servo systems, involving military vehicle power supplies, trials and analysis.
—Management of software review aspects.
—Chairman of Engineering design reviews.

*1986 to 1988*

Engineering Manager
Aircraft Systems Ltd.

—Group project management of six Sonar Development projects, site and trials work, and studies of various sizes. Total responsibility for thirty engineers, including personnel related tasks.
—High level contractual and technical customer liaison and internal liaison including marketing, and business management.
—Quality management.
—Member of factory management team.
—Bid Management, including contract responsibility.

*1988 to Date*

Contract Technical Manager
Self-Employed

—Systems Engineering, and consultation of production and product development aspects of photographic studio systems.

—Design of management control and profitability systems.
—Design of financial control and budgeting systems (including management accounting/cash flow control).
—Consultation on production, and pricing strategy.
—Proposal bid and design and development of visual display controller test equipment. Including production and testing.
—Proposal Bids for various design contracts for power supply systems. Including liaison with customers and generation of technical specifications.
—Management of production engineering for the PCB assemblies of a visual display controller system.
—Proposal bid and manufacture of infrared communication system test equipment.

**Example 1—Comments**
This is a typical tombstone resume and it can be seen immediately that whilst the information is all there, the potential employer really has to work hard to get at what he or she needs to know to make the important "must see" decision. Here are just some obvious areas for improvements:

1. There is nothing the employer can buy on the first page. It is all personal details and training, most of which is not relevant to the position being sought.
2. The tombstone layout means that information required by the employer is on the last page.
3. More space is devoted to what was done in the first job 1974 to 1975 than in 1986 to 1988.
4. The job information is all features with little quantification and certainly no benefits.
5. Bald statements such as "Quality Management" do not mean anything. The employer does not have a crystal ball.
6. Not much thought has been given to the ranking of the responsibilities either in terms of what a potential employer might find exciting or in terms of categories. Engineering and management responsibilities are jumbled up.

## EXAMPLE 2

GREG JONES
100 Hill Street
Los Angeles, CA
90069
818-555-1234

**PROFILE**

A professionally qualified and highly experienced HUMAN RESOURCES SPECIALIST with extensive knowledge and skills in Training and Development, Recruitment and Selection, Career Counselling, Communications and Employee Relations, gained in a wide range of industrial and commercial areas. Additionally, has organized and lectured on personnel and industrial management courses, specializing in organizational behavior.

**KEY SKILLS**

- Identifying training and development needs and developing appropriate strategies in support of corporate objectives.
- Designing, developing and implementing training modules and interactive video programs, with an increasing emphasis on management and sales training, and undertaking post-course validation.
- Managing substantial human and financial resources, including a department of 25 staff and an annual budget of $3 million.
- Initiating and producing a wide range of training modules, and presenting to all levels of management, up to and including board level.
- Determining and developing management development and succession planning, through management audit, performance reviews and career counselling.
- Selecting and recruiting managerial staff across all

functions and disciplines, using psychometric testing and Assessment Center methodology.
- Lecturing to college students and external managers on a wide range of personnel and related business subjects.

## PROFESSIONAL QUALIFICATIONS

FELLOW OF THE INSTITUTE OF PERSONNEL MANAGEMENT (FIPM)

MEMBER OF THE INSTITUTE OF TRAINING AND DEVELOPMENT (MITD)

## CAREER REVIEW—HIGHLIGHTS

**DALSTON BUILDING SOCIETY**          **1980–1992**

TRAINING MANAGER (REGIONS)          1989–1992

- Created new functions to provide dedicated service to branch network sales force in 375 outlets.
- Recruited and developed training specialists for 12 regional offices.
- Designed and introduced a portfolio of business development courses, including customer care, sales and territory planning, cross selling, lead general and sales presentation skills.
- Developed customized training modules to meet specific local needs.
- Managed team of 25 specialist and support staff.

TRAINING AND DEVELOPMENT
MANAGER          1988–1989

- Created and introduced an appraisal system for all levels of staff, linked to a performance related pay system, and fostering an achievement oriented culture.

- Designed and implemented training courses for assessors, specifically supervisors and above.
- Initiated interactive video as major training medium and produced IV programs on a variety of subjects, including a BIVA award winning program on "Assertiveness."
- Managed team of 25 training professionals, with a budget in excess of $2 million.

## MANAGEMENT TRAINING
MANAGER                                                    1985–1988

- Established training as key strategic activity and as a vehicle for cultural and organizational change.
- Developed a new approach to management training, employed TA and other techniques, using cost effective overseas venues.
- Delivered a series of one week intensive programs to all management staff, including senior managers and directors.
- Marketed and sold courses externally to offset internal costs.

## PERSONNEL MANAGER                                        1979–1985

- Managed and developed a team of 9 personnel professionals and over 62 support staff to cover all personnel activities.
- Recruited and selected specialist management staff, for all functional areas.
- Handled and resolved all disciplinary matters referred upwards, sanctioning dismissal where appropriate and managing appeals procedure.
- Undertook salary surveys, recommended level of annual award and negotiated with Staff Association on conditions of service and benefits.

## DALSTON AND LINDFIELD CAREERS SERVICES                              1974–1979

DIVISIONAL CAREERS OFFICER

- Managed and developed 11 professional staff in 3 office locations.
- Determined and implemented annual career counselling and job placement strategy.
- Liaised with careers teachers and lecturers and provided in-service training.
- Provided careers counselling and advice to students and their parents.

Previous personnel experience gained in a variety of roles from 1966–73, with HILL SAMUEL, IPC BUSINESS PRESS, NESTLE and MEDICAL RESEARCH COUNCIL. This included employee relations, recruitment and selection and specific project work.

### EDUCATION AND TRAINING

LONDON SCHOOL OF ECONOMICS
Postgraduate Diploma in Personnel Management
1971–1972
SUSSEX COLLEGE FOR THE CAREERS SERVICE
Diploma in Careers Guidance and Counselling 1973–1974

### INTERESTS

Amateur Dramatics; Rugby; Archery; English History; Film Production

## Example 2—Comments

What makes this resume interesting is the skills summary at the beginning. What is not immediately apparent is that he is not a graduate, although you would expect the sorts of jobs he has done would have such a requirement. This resume shows what can be done to display your skills in the most acceptable way to a prospective employer.

**EXAMPLE 3**

RICHARD JOHNSON
B.Sc.(Hons), Dip W., MIXX, MIYY
21 Broadway
New York, NY 10001
212-555-1234

**Career Summary:**
A senior marketing professional with significant management experience gained with major US and European high technology multinationals.

An effective thinker and doer offering proven strategic planning, business management and communication skills. Able to work effectively at all levels in organizations with the ability to manage change and achieve commercial profit targets.

Career and Achievements to date:

MARKETING MANAGER,                   Jan 91–present
CUSTOMER SERVICE
FASTGROWTH INC, Smalltown

Responsible for marketing hardware and software services portfolio across ten European countries (>$100M revenue). Managed business development, pricing, competitive analysis and new service development to optimize revenue and customer satisfaction. Developed hardware and software business/pricing models matching revenue to channel and distribution costs. Drove specific marketing programs across Europe. Managed "end of life" process. A significant part of this role involves the management and successful implementation of change.

## SENIOR MARKETING CONSULTANT    Sept 89–Jan 91
## EUROPEAN WHIZZO LTD, Another City

Managed product life cycle and marketing of UNIX/ Open Systems and networking in the US's part of XXX's overall computing strategy. Drove two major product line launches in January and May 90. Was instrumental in increasing market share to 8%. Role involved: pricing; product positioning; formulating competitive strategy for US marketplace. Produced promotional literature. Presented to major retail and government customers and professional bodies. Ran series of sales training courses on the Open Systems marketplace for >100 sales people to prepare them to sell these systems to Fortune 500 companies. Marketing responsibility for direct and government sales channels. Drove "Open Systems" message and management interface with X/Open and the DTI.

## PRODUCT MARKETING MANAGER    Mar 88–Sept 89
## LARGE MULTINATIONAL LTD, Greenville

Responsible for development and implementation of marketing strategies for graphics products in UK and Ireland and was the primary communications channel between the USA and UK. Conceived and developed new market segments for graphic product—office automaton and process control. Managed OEM and VAR channels for these segments.

## SYSTEMS SUPPORT MANAGER    May 85–Mar 88
## LARGE MULTINATIONAL LTD, Greenville

Built and managed support business with full P&L responsibility, providing pre- and post-sales support for computer aided design tools for the largest customer base outside the USA. Business was consistently managed within budget meeting both revenue and cost objectives.

1987 revenues—$500K. Success came through effective presentation to senior US management, customers, business partners. Negotiated a $350K system hardware and software upgrade contract. Defined contract terms and conditions and produced sales support material. Successfully set up the US care users' group. Promoted to Product Marketing Manager.

**TECHNICAL SUPPORT MANAGER**  Oct 84–May 85
**LARGE MULTINATIONAL LTD**, Greenville

Turned round a troubled sales organization in 8 months by setting up a formal software support operation for micro-processor development products running on UNIX and VMS hosts. Raised customer satisfaction levels sufficient to increase and retain repeat sales business from the installed base. Promoted to Systems Support Manager.

**SENIOR ENGINEER**
**COMPUTER COMPANY**, London  Oct 81–Oct 84

Supported PDPII and VAX range of processors and VMS, RSXII & RSTS/E operating systems. Performed a consultancy role within the support group. Deputized for the group manager to run the day-to-day operations. Additional responsibility for the sale of processor and disk upgrades to the installed base (value $100K) led to an offer of a position as sales executive with target of $1.6M.

**ENGINEER**
**COMPUTER COMPANY**, London  May 80–Oct 81

Account responsible for 20 major sites. Achieved consistently high levels of customer satisfaction as measured by customer surveys. Promoted to Senior Engineer.

SYSTEMS ENGINEER
PROCESS INDUSTRY LTD, Oiltown     July 78–May 80

Position encompassed all aspects of pre-sales support, customer presentations, project management, in-house acceptance and on-site commissioning of high value process control systems in the Oil, Chemical, Pharmaceutical, Power and Water industries, worldwide. Member of the launch team for XXXX systems. Commissioned the first customer systems.

DESIGN ENGINEER
PROCESS INDUSTRY LTD, Oiltown     July 76–July 78

Designed analog and digital electronics, microprocessors/microsequenced control systems, telemetry systems and interfaces to PDPII and PDP8 processors. Promoted to Systems Engineer.

### Professional and Personal information:

**Professional:**    Diploma in something professional
Education establishment 1989
Member of Professional Institution XX
Member of Professional Institution YY
Won the xxxxxxxxxx Award for 1990

**Qualifications:**    B.Sc. (Hons), Electronic Engineering
Good University 1976

**Training:**    Progressive management training
including:
Marketing, Product Marketing, Direct
Marketing, Professional Selling Skills,
Presentation Skills, Finance, Time
Management, Project Management,
Problem Solving (Advantage &

|            | Analytical Trouble Shooting), Team Building |
|------------|---------------------------------------------|
|            | Various technical training courses covering hardware, software and networking. |
| **Outside Interests:** | Elected Chairman of xxxxxxxxxx Club 1989–1991 |
|            | Elected Secretary of xxxxxxxxxx Club 1988–1989 |
|            | Photography, Bridge, Skiing |

## Example 3—Comments

Despite using prose, rather than bullet points, this resume works well. Some of the better points worth mentioning include:

1. The first page includes the career summary. Personally I am not too taken with front pages because it makes the resume into at least three pages. However here the candidate has included his career summary so that there is something the employer can buy on the first page.
2. Job title is given before the employer and before the dates of the jobs held. Just as well really, because this applicant does not stay in jobs for long. By putting dates on the right hand the jobs tenure, or the lack of it, is not so obvious.
3. Job achievements decrease as we are taken back through the employment history, thus reducing unnecessary information yet having the effects of highlighting current skills and achievements.

EXAMPLE 4

Dominic David Jobs
5 Navarino Grove
Akron, Ohio 11111
401-555-1234

Has strong technical background including Unix, C, Networks and Graphics and good communication and presentation skills, and a deep understanding of the Unix industry, products and markets. Looking for a role that includes significant customer contact, with the opportunity to contribute to produce and corporate strategy.

## Career to date

European Graphics Marketing Manager,
Fastgrowth Europe Inc.                    3 yrs

Representing Europe's requirements in Corporate, and providing leadership to the country marketing and sales organizations. Activities include customer presentations, major account support, press interviews, non-disclosure presentations, etc. Projects include product introductions and transitions, a server market study (with KPMG) and collateral production, and magazine articles. Contributions made in product positioning and corporate strategy presentations. Covered most product areas in addition to graphics.

Pre-Sales Technical Consultant,
Fastgrowth USA Inc                    4.5 yrs

I was the eleventh employee at Fastgrowth, the third software person. Initially covered pre- and post-technical support, specializing in Windows, Graphics and Networking. Presented to customers on many technical and strategic areas, and gave some of the early customer and internal training classes. Became the presenter of choice in many subject areas. Installed most of Fastgrowth internal UNIX systems in the early days. Built the European portion of Fastgrowth's XXX/IP wide area network.

Development Engineer, Help Co.
(Medical Electronics)                                    6.5 yrs

System, electronics and software design. Later consulting on all development projects. Designed (still) the best selling EMG (neurological diagnostics equipment). Short stay in marketing to launch the product. Introduced C and Unix as the development environment.

Development Engineer, Kind Devices
(Industrial Electronics)                                    2 yrs

Electronics and software design. Also sys admin & RPG programming of IBM S/32.

Production Test Engineer, Transecon
(Test and Management)                                    1 yr

Fault finding and calibration of product units.

Lab Technician, New Band
(Bare PCB manufacture)                                    9 months

Maintenance of etch and plating chemical processes.

**Example 4—Comments**

What is good here includes:

1. All the information fits in less space.
2. This candidate in fact has no formal degree in engineering or computing but has obviously held jobs requiring graduate if not post-graduate status. The education section is omitted but the experience speaks for itself.

# EXAMPLE CAREER STATEMENTS

How these are constructed is outlined on page 35. Some Careers Advisers and many head hunters, it should be noted, do not approve of the Career Statements because they are subjective and represent the applicant's view of themselves. In my experience employers find them useful. This is ambiguous and confusing but, as was stated in the beginning of the book, there are no absolute rules. You, the reader, will have to decide.

## SECRETARIAL AND ADMINISTRATIVE

Experienced executive secretary. Able to work independently and make decisions. Proven administration and organization ability, supported by good interpersonal skills. Used to working with executive management at the highest level.

A technically aware sales co-ordinator who has good communication and organizational skills, able to work at all levels, is committed and can work on her own initiative.

Enthusiastic Customer Service Co-ordinator with proven ability to control multiple marketing projects within given timescales whilst maintaining a high quality of work and achievement of set goals. A confident communicator both internally and externally.

A reliable, conscientious and loyal administrator with good secretarial, accounting and purchasing skills. A skilled negotiator of office equipment and supplies.

## MIDDLE AND SENIOR MANAGEMENT

An experienced bi-lingual (English-German) Industrial Designer with an extensive knowledge of the xxx industry. Particularly strong aesthetic skills combine with a developed understanding of manufacturing requirements and commercial reality.

A qualified and motivated Health Manager who is an innovator with a proven record of achievement in implementing change successfully, founded on a comprehensive experience within the health sector from nursing to management strategy.

A highly experienced, motivated Management Accountant with comprehensive career within the Retail and Leisure industry, wishing to pursue his career in an environment where his financial and inter-personal skills will make a positive contribution.

A professional geologist with excellent experience in exploration, basin synthesis, together with sub-surface operations supported by a good knowledge of contractor services and offering proven skills in data base design and management.

Human resource manager with recently developed business analysis—information systems—ability, seeks a human resource management role with an opportunity to develop general management and information management interests in a healthcare context.

## EXECUTIVE AND DIRECTORS

A self motivated and achievement orientated Financial Controller/Director with strong business development skills and a proven record of profit improvement through planning and implementing financial and MIS strategies.

An experienced international general manager with an outstanding track record of maximizing start-up opportunities in highly competitive high technology markets through her high energy, creativity, and a capacity for making things happen.

A confident and creative manager with a proven record of achievement in general and technical management with multinational companies.

A natural team leader in a changing environment with a relaxed style to achieving set goals through the development and motivation of people.

A successful General Manager with Sales and Marketing experience, she utilizes a modern, energetic, versatile and customer oriented style. She advocates teamwork, quality and delegation to build winning profitable companies.

# FEEDBACK

Theory is all right but it is no substitute for the real thing.

Please write and tell us:

- What you think
- Which resumes you thought were good (if you receive them)
- What worked for you and what did not (if you are a job hunter)
- Any points or tips you would like us to pass on
- What sections need improving

or anything that you think will contribute to making the book even more "perfect".

Send your feedback to:
Max A. Eggert
c/o Century Business
Random House
20 Vauxhall Bridge Road
London SW1V 2SA

# ABOUT THE AUTHOR

## MAX A. EGGERT
MA, BSc, AKC Psychol, FIPM, MITD

Max Eggert first read Theology before transferring his allegiance to Psychology and then to Industrial Relations.

He is Managing Partner of Eggert & Eggert, an international consultancy dedicated to Human Resources Management and Outplacement. Many thousands of individuals at all levels and backgrounds have benefited their careers by working with Max who works in the UK and internationally as a strategist and as an adviser to organizations who retain his services.

Max is married with two children, lives in Sussex and London, and is a priest in the Diocese of Chichester. His current passion is riding his gray cob.